This Book Belongs To

_ _

_ _

_ _

Copyright Page

Kheru Nefer Kings and Queens Names and Hieroglyphs Coloring Book
©2021 Shaaim Family LLC

All rights reserved. No portion of this book may be reproduced, stored in a retrieval system or
transmitted an any for or by any means -electronic, mechanical, photocopy, recording,
or any other – except for brief quotation in printed reviews, without the permission of the publisher.

Published by: Our Communities Our Children Publishing LLC, 1205 Atlantic Avenue, Brooklyn, N.Y. 11216
Website: www.OCOCbooks.com
A children's history book about ancient Egypt (Kemet).
Author: Obi Shaaim Maa
Cover: Metu Degg Khet
Graphics: Metu Degg Khet
ISBN: 978-1-953952-20-2

Name	Djoser	Hetephernebti
Hieroglyphs		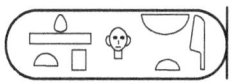
Phonetic	Zosar	Hetep-her-nebti
Transliteration	Djsr	Htp-hr-nebti
Meaning	(Sacred)	(Peace upon the provider)

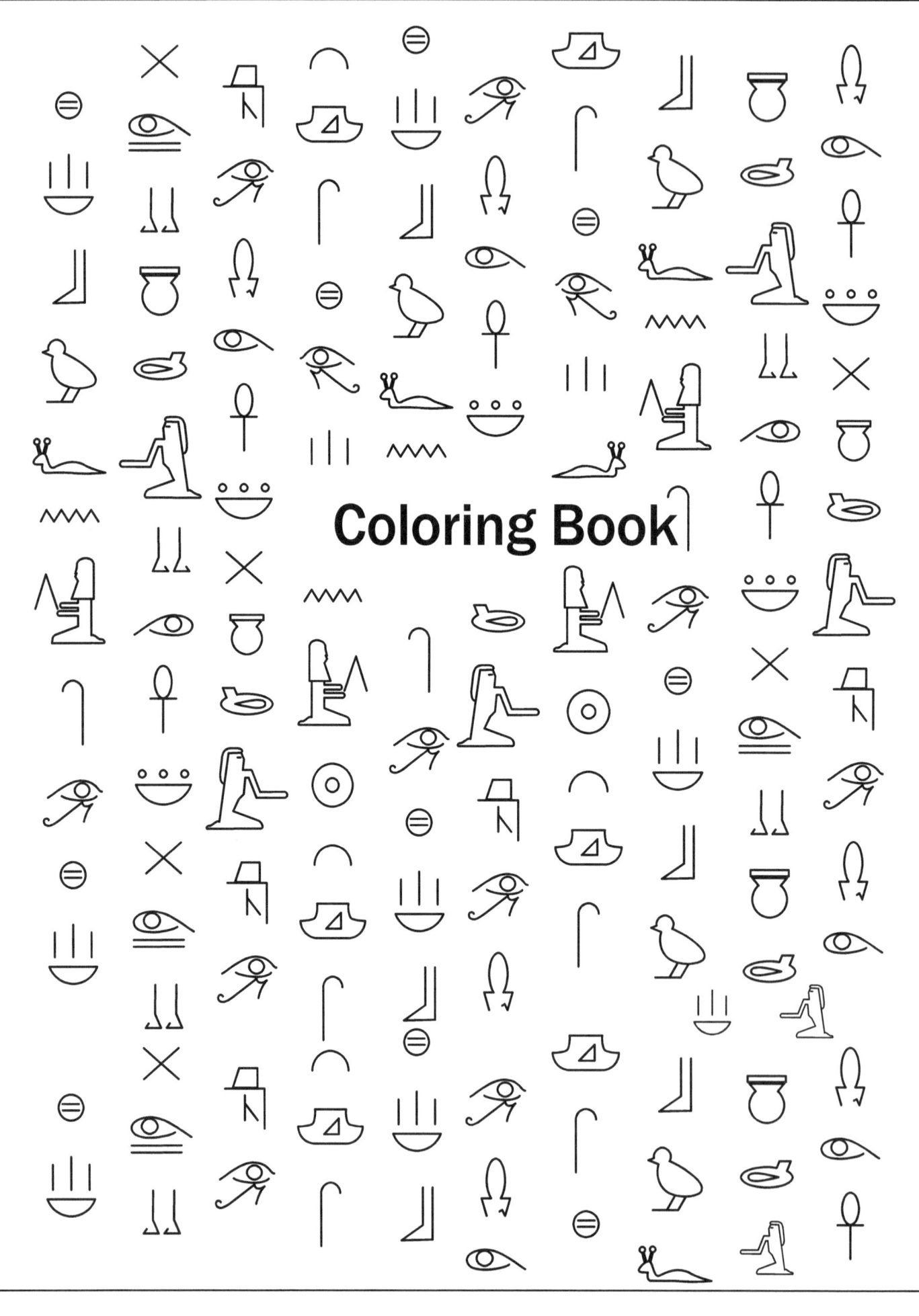

Name	Khufu	Henutsen
Hieroglyphs		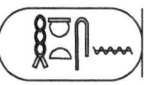
Phonetic	Koo-fu	Hen-nut-sen
Transliteration	Khufu	HNutSen
Meaning	(Protector)	(Sister Wife)

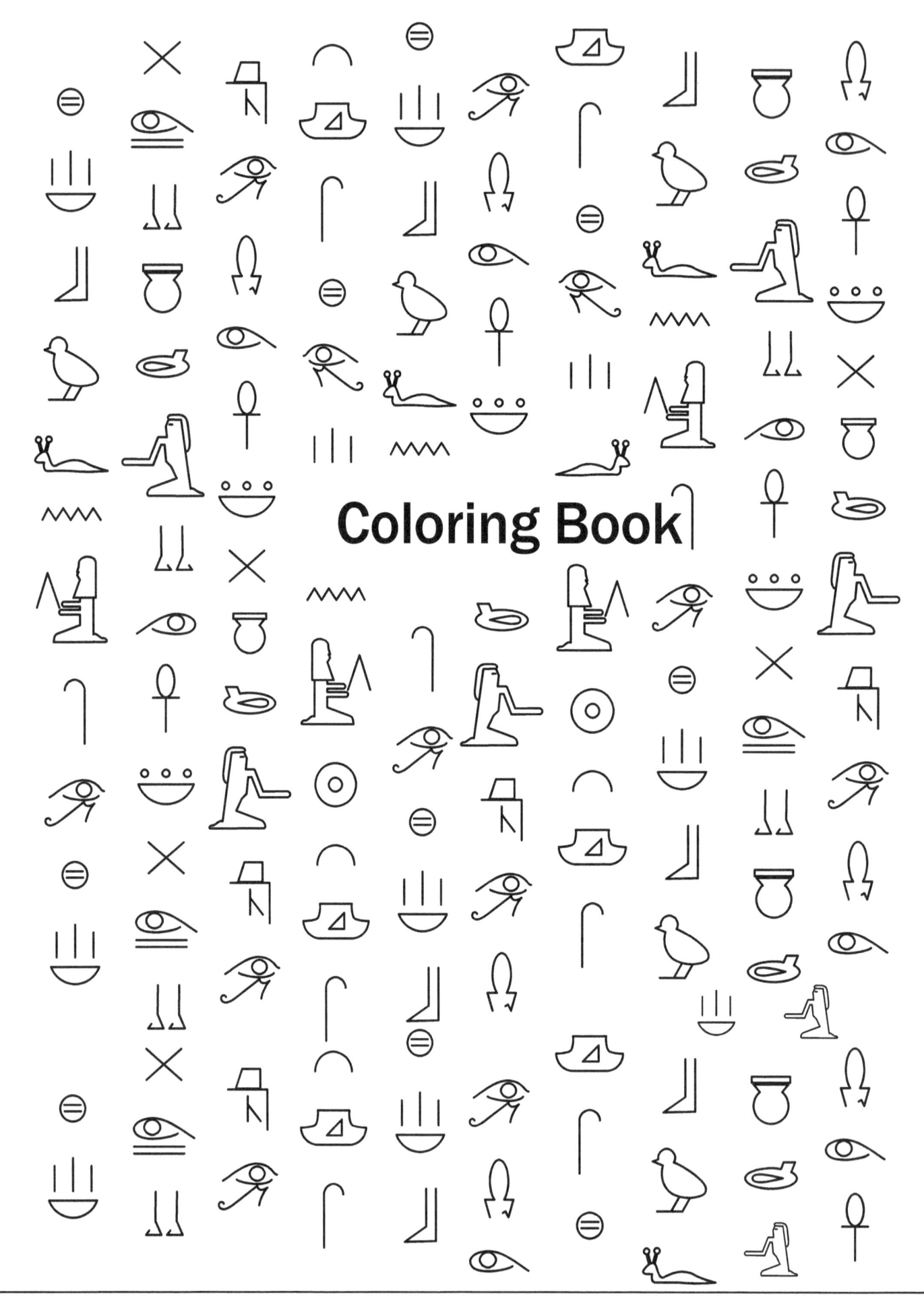

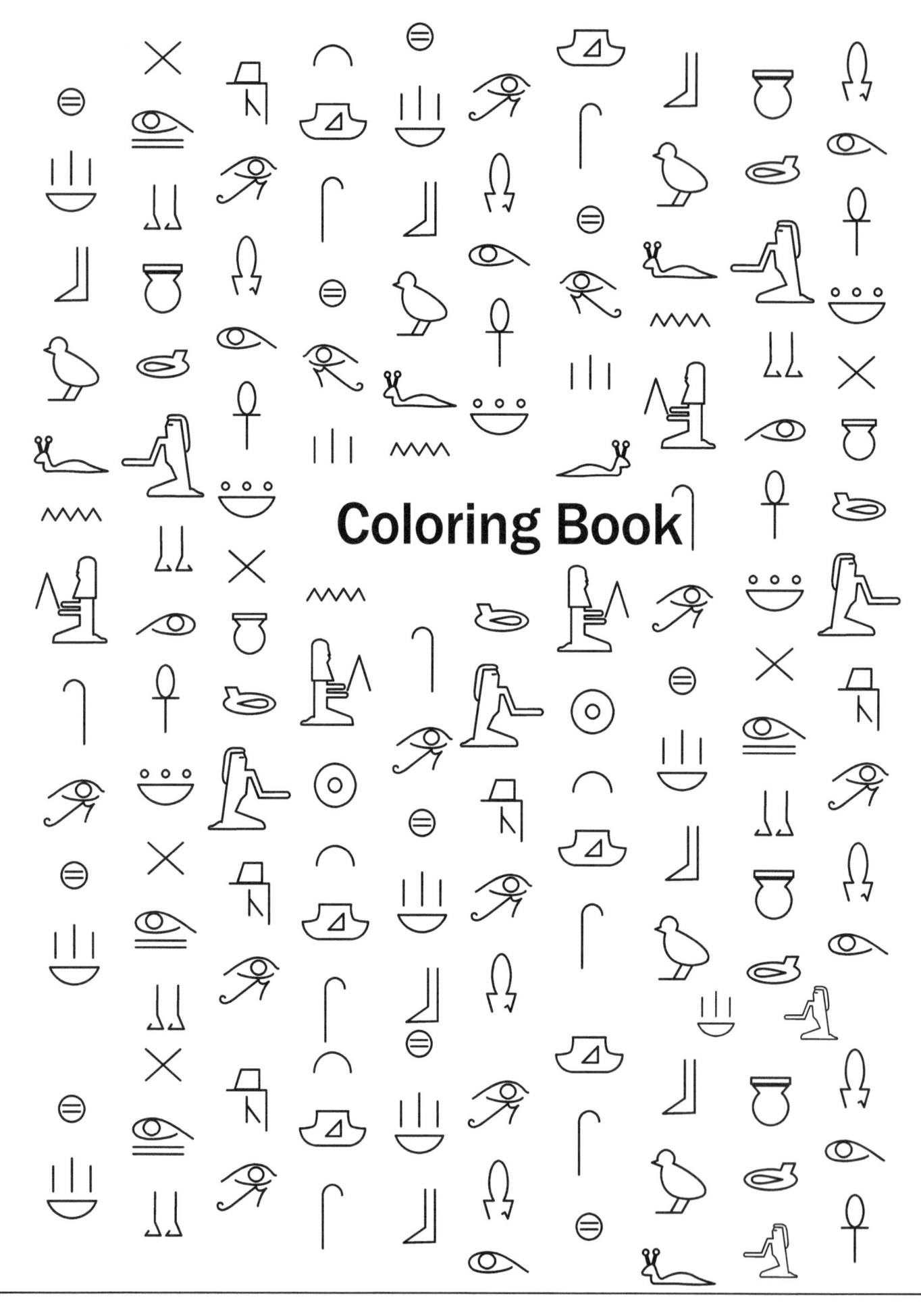

Name	Thutmose II	Hatshepsut
Hieroglyphs		
Phonetic	Tehuti Mes	Hat-Shepsut
Transliteration	Thti Ms	Ht Shpst
Meaning	(Tehuti's child)	(Formost of the ancestors)

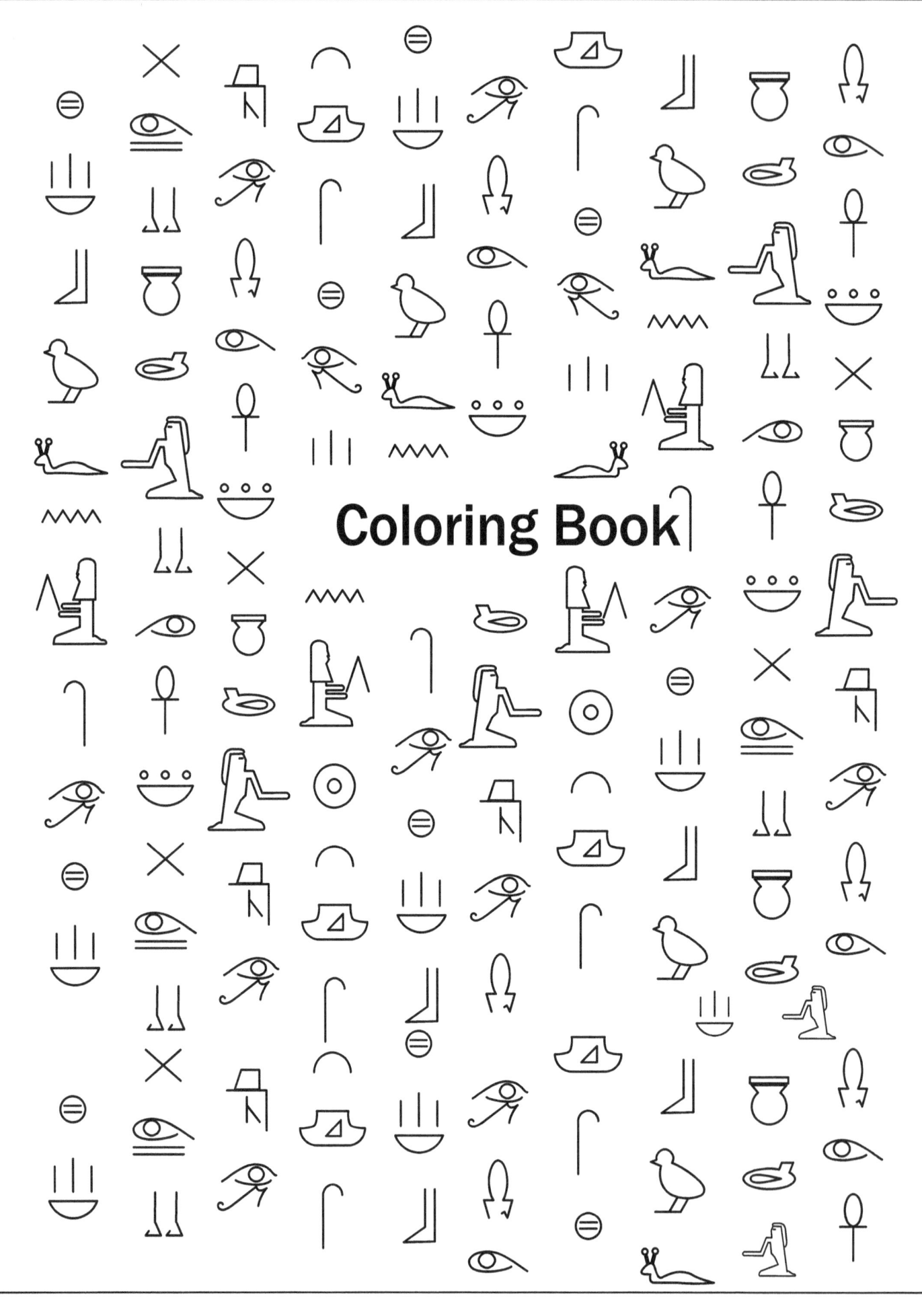

Name	Ahmose-Nefertari	Ahmose
Hieroglyphs		
Phonetic	Ahmes Nefertari	Ahmes
Transliteration	Ah-Ms Nfrtri	Ah-Ms
Meaning	(Moon child's beautiful companion)	(Moon child)

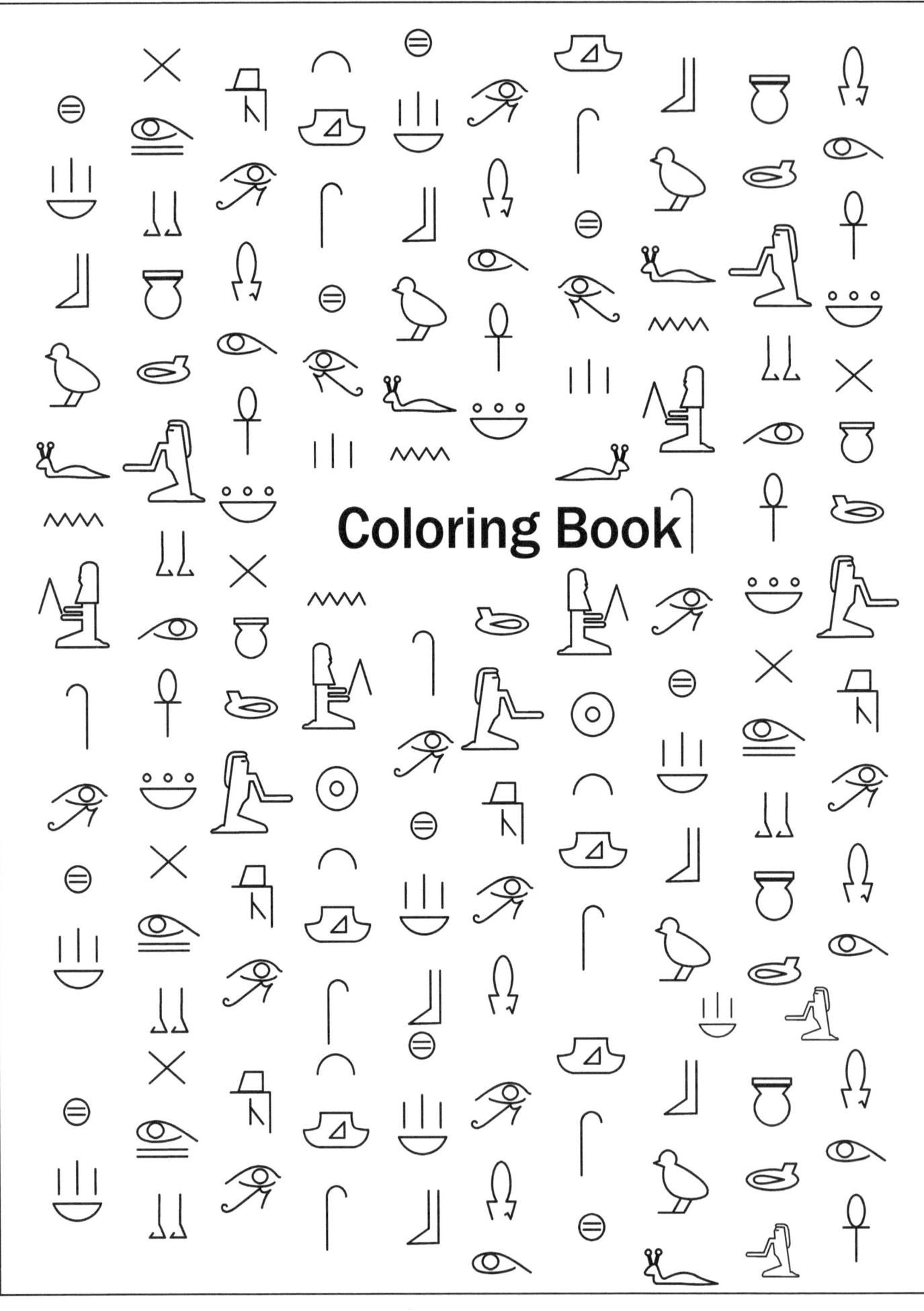

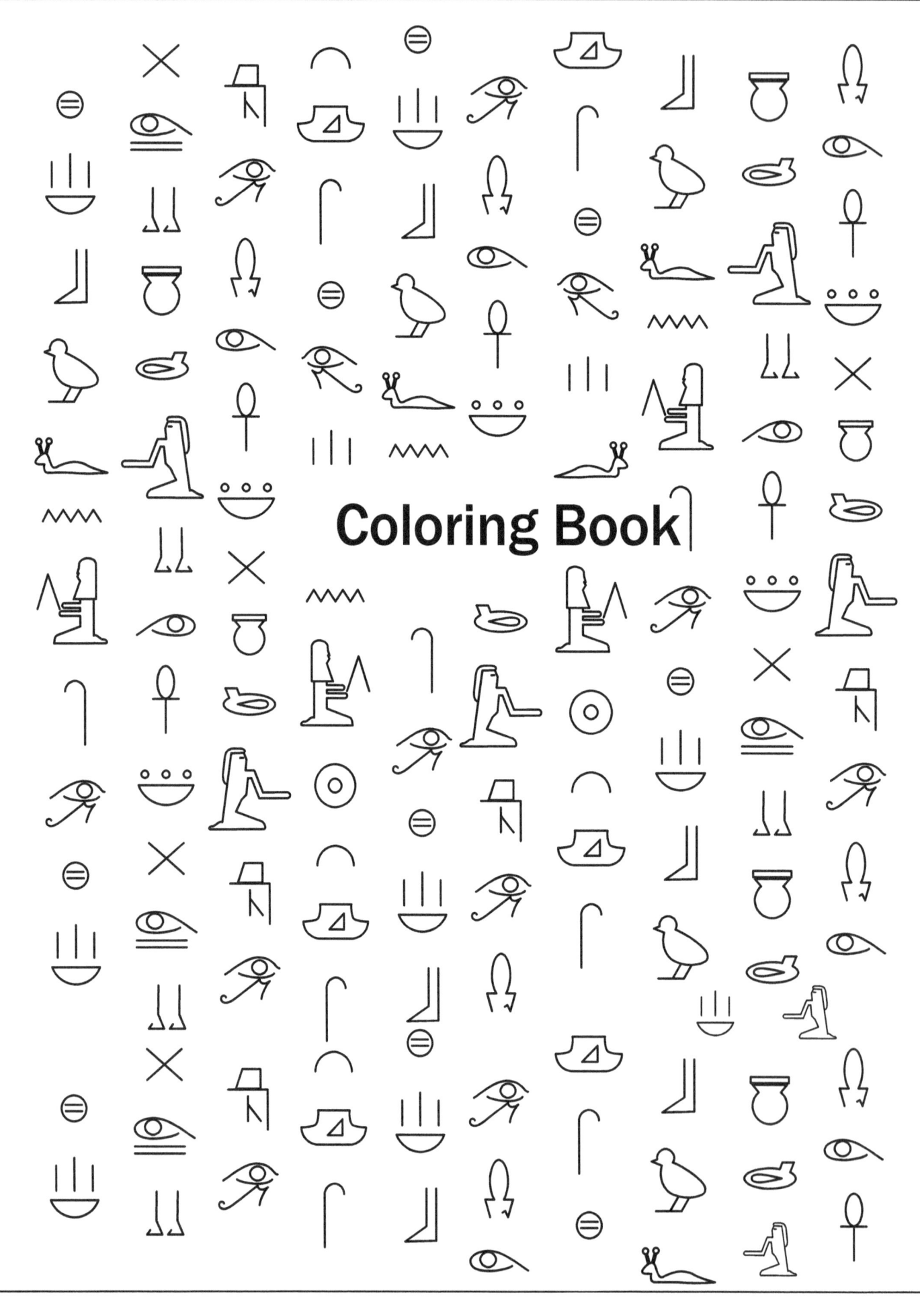

Name	Neferu III	Senusret I
Hieroglyphs		
Phonetic	Nefer u	Sen-un-Useret
Transliteration	Nifru	Usrt-Sn
Meaning	(Beautifully Great)	(Powerful Brother)

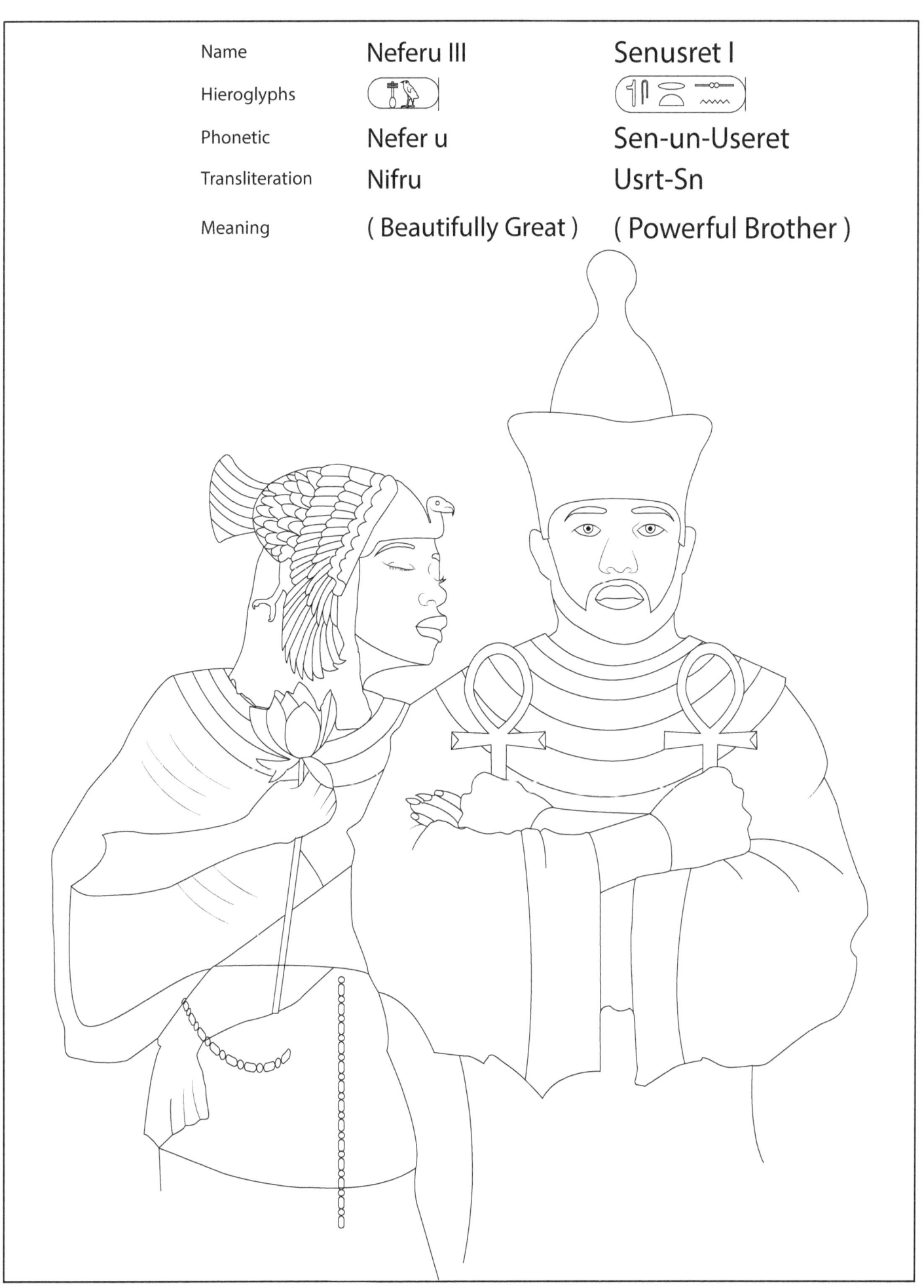

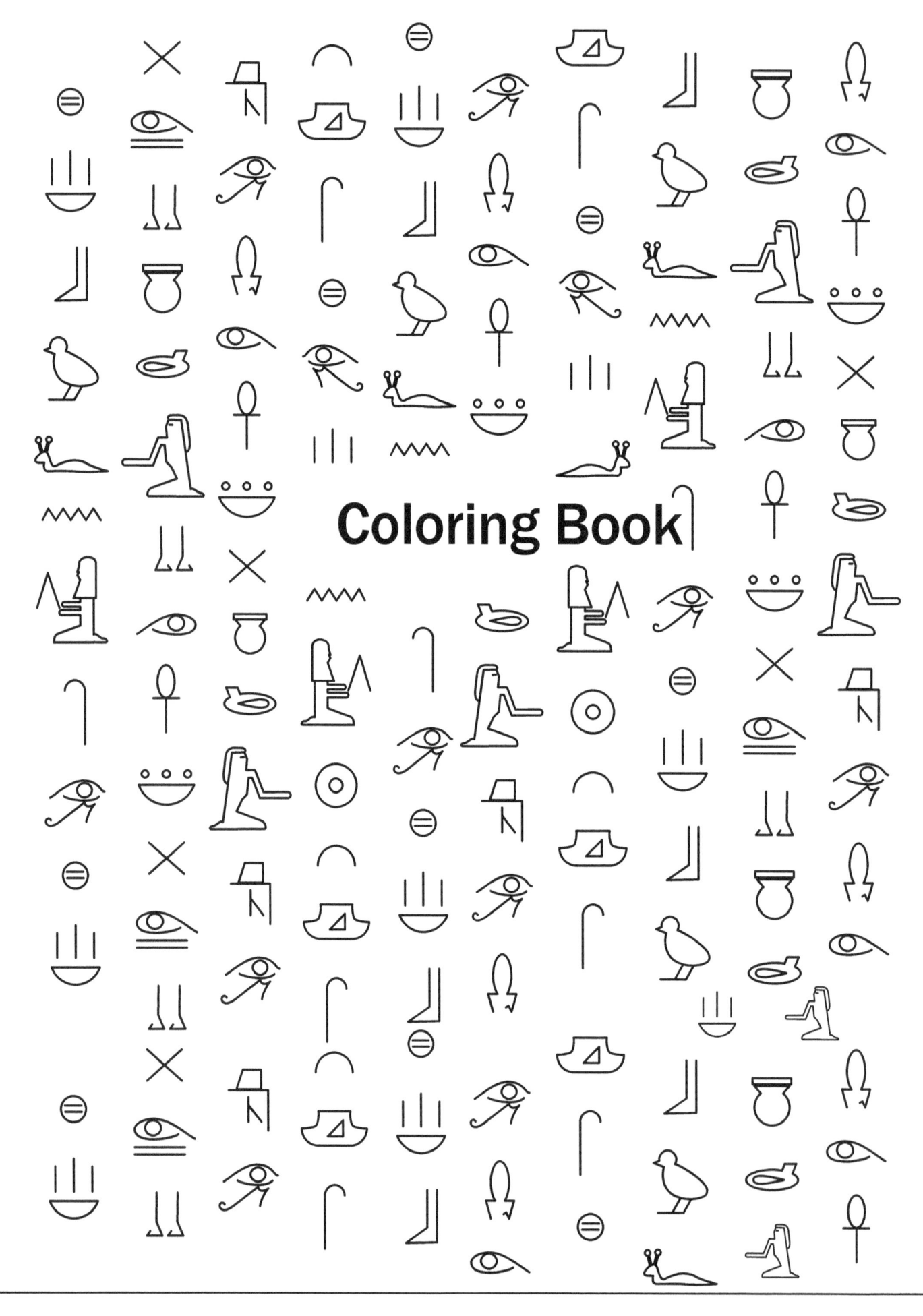

Name	Thutmose III	Merytre-Hatshepsut I
Hieroglyphs	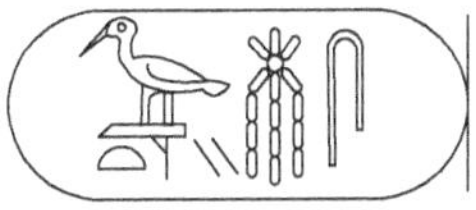	
Phonetic	Tehuti-Mes	Meru Ra-Hat-Shepsut
Transliteration	Thti-Ms	Mru-Ra-Ht-Shpst
Meaning	(Tehuti's Child)	(Beloved of Ra Formost of ancestors)

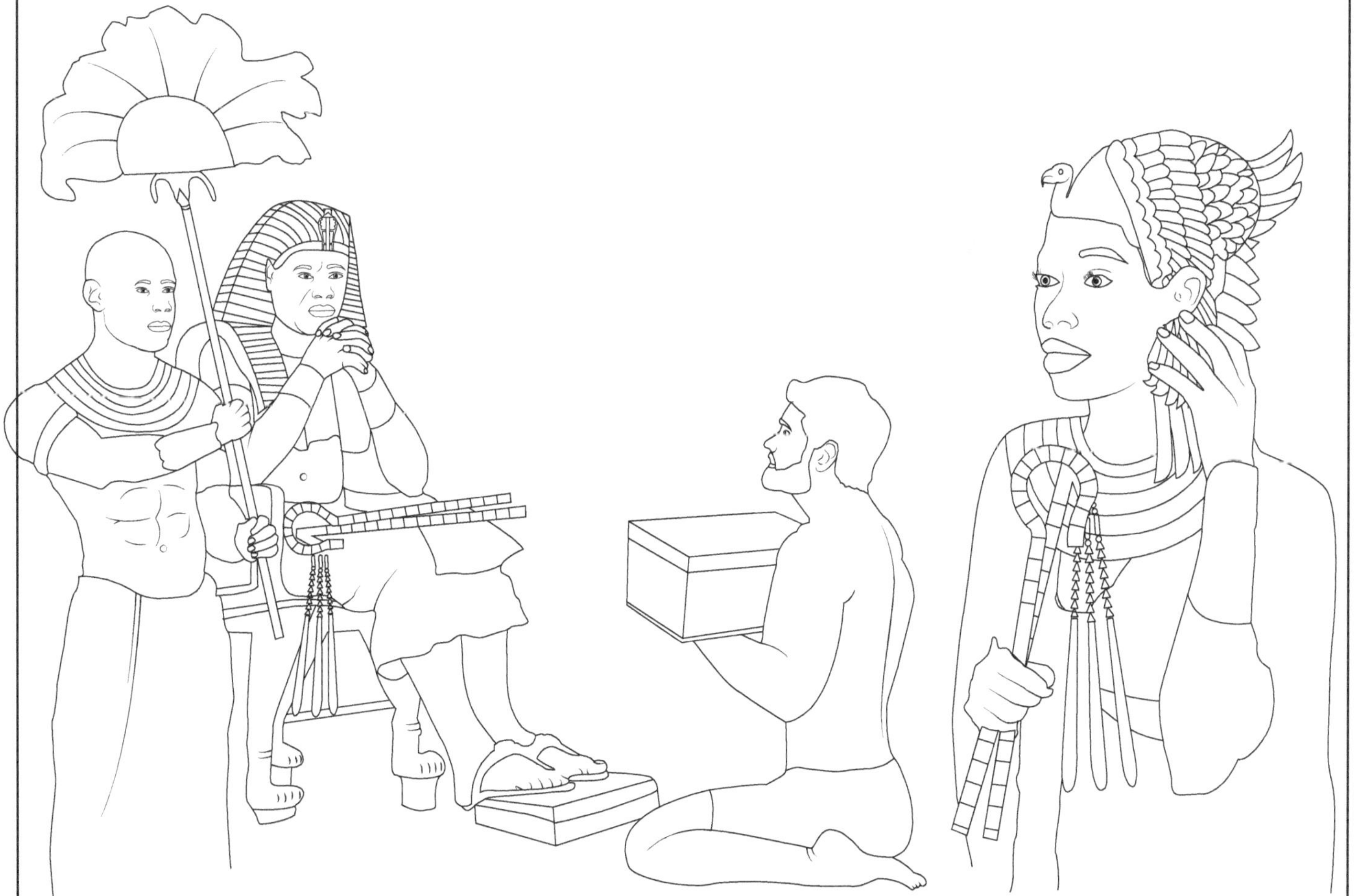

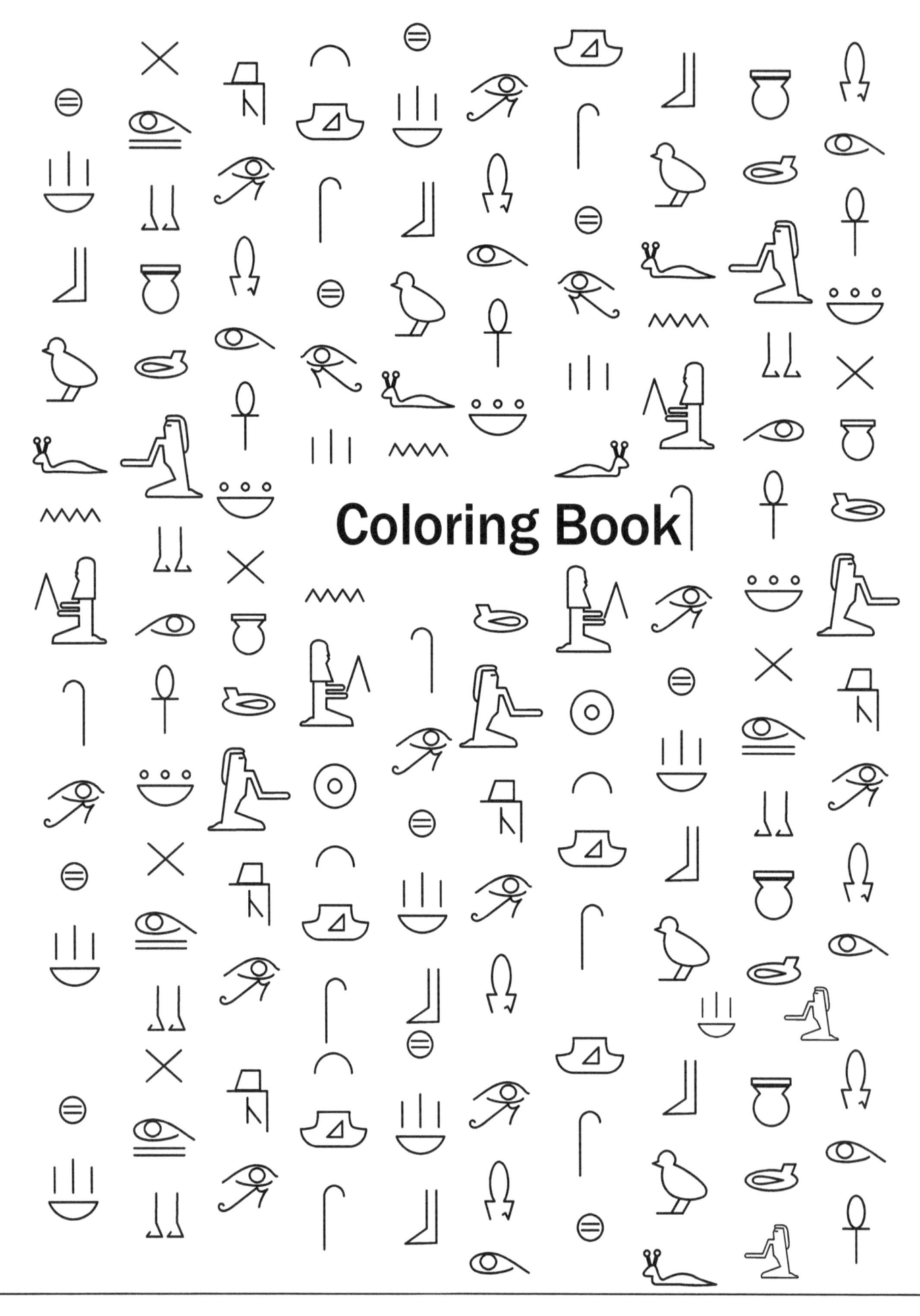

Name	Neferthenut		Senusret III
Hieroglyphs			
Phonetic	Nefert Henut		Sen-nu-sret
Transliteration	Nfrt-Hut		Usrt-Sn
Meaning	(Beautifully seving Nut)		(Powerful Brother)

Kheru Nefer: Beautiful Night: (Kings and Queens) is history, music, dance and art packaged in the patterned, predictable and rhythmic harmonies of a fun-filled children's book.
This addition to the Kheru Nefer: Beautiful Night series features 11 king and queen pairs who held their relationships together in order to hold a nation together.
Their enduring accomplishments are brought back so your child (Children) can enjoy and learn. To get the the childrens history book and other Kheru Nefer products, go to:

OCOCBooks.com or your favorite online book store.

www.ingramcontent.com/pod-product-compliance
Lightning Source LLC
Chambersburg PA
CBHW080014090526
44578CB00014B/856